Balancing
The Scales

'A Journey Of Recovery'

I0103895

Christine Khisa

chipmunkapublishing
the mental health publisher

All rights reserved, no part of this publication may be reproduced by any means, electronic, mechanical photocopying, documentary, film or in any other format without prior written permission of the publisher.

Published by
Chipmunkapublishing
PO Box 6872
Brentwood
Essex CM13 1ZT
United Kingdom

http://www.chipmunkapublishing.com

Copyright © Christine Khisa 2012

Edited by Aleks Lech

ISBN   978-1-84991-805-3

Chipmunkapublishing gratefully acknowledge the support of Arts Council England.

Acknowledgements

I would like firstly give my utmost thanks to my children Michelle, Amie, Jessica and Reuben, for their patience and understanding whilst I organised the material for this Anthology of poems. I would like to additionally thank them for their assistance in processing the work.

I would like to thank Miss Munroe, an English teacher who encouraged me to read and had faith in my ability.

I thank London South Bank University, and Middlesex University Health and Social Care Faculties, namely John, , Kate, Wendy and Trish for the support, encouragement, motivation and confidence building enabled through the process of Service User Involvement opportunities, allowed me to realise skills and potential that had remained dormant for many years and in so doing, had a positive impact on my mental well being and continuing recovery.

I am thankful for the many Service User Peers that I had the good fortune to work with.

Finally I would like to acknowledge with respect and dedicate this book to my parents Joseph Khaemba Khisa (Deceased) and Susanna Muhindi, for allowing me this opportunity to express myself.

Once called 'a Jack of all trades', by my father, I reply
' Ego can Ego mos tamen tendo'
(I can, I will but try)

Dedicated to my children, their children and their children's children, a legacy of the view through the window of my experience.
Miss Kristene Khaemba Khisa

Balancing The Scales

Poetry a medium for dialogue and transition

Nubian

'Empress to all, object of desire, the will to nurture, the will to inspire.'

Mothers

'You hold the wealth of nations in the palms of your hands.'

Fathers

'Sons, do not as I do but as I advise, let my obstacles in life not be repeated in yours.'

Children

'The legacies of today will be borne by the children of tomorrow.'

Motivation

'If chance is an opportunity, then there needs be opportunity for chance.'

Well Being

'Well being is on a polarised continuum, where mental illness is not always a constant.'

Education and The Globalised Child

Once denied

Then a privilege

Now a prerequisite

Now an entitlement

It must be a right

'Education for all.'

Depression

'Mental illness is not the sum of the whole, but a fraction in the equation that is life.'

Loss

'Do not only mourn the loss, but celebrate the legacy of those who have passed on.'

Recovery

An endless journey with different routes, sometimes one must alight on the journey and then continue at a time when able.

The Individual

'To cater for the majority establishes a minority and vice versa creates a dichotomy. Equality is not about sameness, it is about meeting individual needs.'

Communication

'Music is universal and transcends all boundaries, harmonies to soothe the soul and words for most to hear. Do not let language and culture be a barrier to progress.'

Creative thoughts

'Open your mind and do not limit your creativity, it's within all of us, it is for you to find it and nourish it. Create the mood, the atmosphere and the serenity, the creativity will follow. Be your own judge of your creative potential.'

Balancing the Scales

Mother Nature was so called
Because of the responsibility it unfolds
Women of the world have much accountability
Balancing the scales of domesticity
Some mothers, role models, professionals, employees
Whilst also rearing the next generation
Who will soon take the reins from the generation before

Women instil in society the caring element that creates
foundations
Holding the threads of community
They are the heart of the nation
Bringing forth new life to a world centuries old
Our positions more prominent as progress unfolds

We teach and nurture, instil, inspire
Lead and comfort when others tire
We hold you in the palm of our hands
We enable destinies
We bond and calm

We are the world's diplomats
With little recognition
We need tact and diplomacy
In any given situation
The language of motherhood
Is universal across nations
From region to region there needs no explanation

A woman's domain increases with time
As her power unfolds, sometimes status declines
But it is taken in her stride, as a lesson to be learnt
That the work of a woman
Is usually seen but not heard

A Tapestry of Sand

With each grain
Dependent on the other
The sum of the whole
Needs a fraction, a grain
In order to amass
The bulk that is needed
To act as a barrier
A beach or much more
The tide out, it is bared
When in, it's consumed
When quick death defying
Or an ingredient to build
a component of glass
when in hand
soft to touch
with each grain descending
to relative parts on the shore
beneath my feet an entity
with volume much more
with the heat of the sun
caresses and invites
with the damp of the rain
or the tide it repels
when buried in jest
its volume is felt
with its weight you are motionless
till all is removed
on it castles are built
and loved ones names written in the sand
hearts are given to each other
intertwined on the shore
the footprints it keeps
till the tide beckons
leaving no evidence of there having been
the castles collapse
and the surface is levelled
and nature claims back
the formation of before
the tapestry of sand.

Coping Alone

Insignificance and ignorance
Have long since been my norm
From a very early age
When I ventured into the unknown
Allow me the opportunity
To be as I choose to be
Do not inflict on me opinions
Of so called normality
Whilst not a danger to myself
And neither those that I care for
My danger the environment
The inhumanity it affords
When children die unnecessarily
Whilst governments abide
At what point are chance and opportunity
A given as a child when whilst compared
Some admit defeat
Where is the like for like
Where is diversity acknowledged
When current norms applied
How does a child told not the norm
Act as such and fit in
In the absence of support and worth

How does the child know to be a child and do like wise
Lest history repeat itself
With every child that matters
A policy I have yet to see in my child's experience
Is it every child
Or is choice applied
Some matter more than others
When once a child now not a child
But as an adult wiser
What knowledge can a parent impart
When hands are tied in seeking
Help and support
To educate and grow
Said child into a responsible being
To contribute to society
To be part of a community
To be an upstanding individual
And proud of his ethnicity
To lead not to follow
By example and much more
It should be a right not privilege
Is there need for more policy to dictate
What should be a natural phenomenon
In any given society to date

Freedom of Expression

If society is my prison
And freedom is the key
I would much rather the insanity
Of me being me
No conversations to adhere to
No values or given norms
No specific culture
Any language, my platform
Universal disciplines
To control order and quell unrest
Did man stop evolving
With the origin of species
Or is it just the physical
That confines reality
The subject of the mind
And the boundaries theory dictates
Any deviance from the expected
Another label attached to date
Supposition without dialogue
Is regression none the less
An abuse of emotional intelligence
All intellect suppressed
Therapeutic interventions
Applied so publicly
Breaching of such confidences
Worse than the traumas magnified
Of the catalogue of tragedies
A percentage my mind
Whilst lacking in capacity
By failing every measure
The yardstick rule, the norm applied
What happened to measure for measure?

From Father to Son (a message)

Son, do not as I do
But as I advise
As I wish you to avoid
Many obstacles in life
Many I challenged
I can omit from your path
Benefit son
From the legacy of my toils
If I can impart wisdom
Of my life journey to date
This knowledge will lay foundations
On your journey of discovery
Son, be proud, before you make me proud
Do not measure success by financial gain alone
It should be personal to you
Help others hindered by society's ills
Enhance your journey; success will unfold
Enabling the success of your peers
Lead by example and be proud to be

Balancing The Scales

From Mother to Child: A Discussion

Whilst I cannot share all that I know

And that I do still try

Appreciation of my foolish advice

Is never by the by

If but a fraction of success

Is in a word or phrase repeated

In good behaviour on one day

Then I am not defeated

We accept both good and bad

Both Yin and Yang

They why not when it comes to children

For wanting to be cool, for our name

To be known, be called

Then surrounded by a crowd

For being everyone's friend

My foolish advice by way of a quote

From the 'olden days', at the times you

Suggest I came from (LOL)

'A friend to all is a friend to none'

Aristotle 384BC to 322 BC

As my children will gain not only from my pool

Of experiences and disciplines learnt

And when a child learns not to say I can't,

But is given the confidence to say I will try

Then I know there is something I have

Taught and learnt

For which there is no examination

But the test is when a child will say

Mum what do you know about this

Generation

Well the Vikings my son and then we go on

About the pyramids and how they

Might have been constructed

I bring in old Pythagoras

We talk of Galileo Galilei

We talk as we watch the sky at night

But cannot find the way to the local observatory

But we will sometimes talk about how

Many suns or moons may be in the galaxy

I introduce relativity and the apple

Dropping straight down from the tree

When I get out of the pool I say

My bones ache, my son will tell the cause

The gravitational pull and that I am overweight

I am glad I am so good willed

But when he asks me to spell

Sometimes I am lost

Especially when it's Ptolemy

The skills I too had when once a child

Self taught

Now passed to another generation

With gleam I reiterated in the 'olden days',

A phrase my children have frequently mentioned

On the subject of Henry the Eighth

I did not understand as my child had asked

On the basis that when he ate, I ate, I was there to see,

I was at the table

Whilst my concept of time in doubt

When once a child

Some of the doubt is now my children's

I knew of Henry the Eighth, children

But I doubt he knew of me

I know you feel I am old

And long in tooth

And do not know what it is like

For the children of today

That I relearn as you learn

That I read what you read

That I watch the television with you

With a moral of the story to share

If not a principle to consider

That I listen to the songs that you like

Even though I beg you to be selective

When you tell me a song is out of date

When you tell your younger sibling

That a song in the charts three months ago

No one listens to any more

I say choose for yourselves

It is not always a case of what's in

The sacrifices we make as a child

For wanting to be one of the crowd

I will not detract from your fun

Only enhance the fact

That there is something to be learned from

Every situation

If Tom and Jerry can transcend

Boundaries of age, continent and other description

If I could laugh with my child, when I could not laugh as
a child, and forgive anything implied

I am laughing today

At what I remember I saw

But I did not understand

When the formula remains

Relatively the same

Then it's not rocket science

That as I laugh with my children

I remember being a child and found

A connectedness to use as a foundation

If this is what alleviates pressures

In both parents and in children

Balancing The Scales

It's evidence that the little things in life

That give the most pleasure

As uncomfortable as I am in the social setting

What would you do if I said

When asked what I'd been up to

I be proud to say I watched Tom and Jerry, Pink
Panther 2,

I also watched Phineas and Ferb, I had to watch
Hannah Montanna and the sweet life of Zack and Cody

I have to work with the same script

To converse with the angels

I have to demonstrate I still know how it goes

When we watch we laugh, till tears appear

For me the only occurrence

Resulting from this we can communicate

Children tell me what's going on in their lives

Outside the home

We have conversations I never had

But in a poem posthumously entitled

'a conversation with my father'

Whilst I have found voice and will

Now speak my conversation is quite brief

When no confidence is perceived as lack

My lack has been addressed

To my children all four

Over the years

Some list the faults when cannot cope

When praising take the glory

My glory is that I can say I have

My children and roll off their names

My glory is when I consider

The blessings as a result I have gained

That there are some less fortunate

That cannot say the same

Awareness of that the facts today

When a child has shared what I enabled

It took me years to learn to spell many words

And years more to forget how

At this point I have poetic licence to add

As a private joke between ourselves

Mum!!!!!

'It's all Greek to me'

Mother: A conversation

I see the sadness in your eyes
The alienation it tries to summarise
You long for the land that you still call home
Even though distant from where your children have grown
You speak in a tongue that is not your first
Articulate and fluent in another
You find comfort when you can communicate in the latter
To express your needs
To find words to explain
When using your second tongue there is less familiarity
The struggles that have been your life
Both chapter and verse
Some I have witnessed, some I have heard
You did the jobs that no one would
You worked the shifts that no one took
As one of eight, least heard and said
When your cries were silent
Mine were too
I shed a silent tear
Thinking myself responsible for many of your pains
Not fitting the puzzle of the family frame

Not cut to the dimension
Not part of the sum
Not equating to anything
Other than none
I sought approval, praise even love
I sought a mother's love
Not seeing affection displayed as I grew
Not seeing the warmth that a family drew
Not experiencing connectedness
Not a pea in a pod
But on the periphery
In a world of my own
In a family of one
I existed alone
Now older and wiser I hope, I think
I can now as a mother appreciate your plight
And wish to forgive and be forgiven
For any pain caused
By the indifference and my being
When brought in your domain
I just longed for attention
And to be understood
As I did not understand the vocabulary
That was spoken in the house
As a mother it's hard
To give to all equally
To hear all when they cry
To see all who are happy
Whilst one may still cry
As a mother I wish
Not to repeat which was mine
The experience I had
Having learnt from the past
Will stand my children in good stead
I will not waste that which was by way of experience
Let bygones be bygones
And leave the past laid to rest

For not being there

The rejection I find hard to bear
My soul destroyed
The silence I find deafening
Like the silence you had to bear
When you could not find the words
That you did not want me to hear
I feel isolated
A part of me is missing
There is a void I cannot fill
As you were my first blessing
Forgive me for all the wrongs
I may have been responsible for
Give me a chance
An opportunity to show
Your are worthy of much more
Did I neglect you?
Did I abandon you?
When all I wanted
Were your wounds to heal
For you to have a quality of life
That I could not fulfil
I am not in the least perfect
Especially with my condition
Which I have come to terms with
Although it dominated you whilst a child
It may have scarred your memory
Leaving me in it less than worthwhile
I think of you every day
In my thoughts and deeds and prayers

Every day I am with your siblings
I wish that you too were there
I was supposed to protect, nurture, guide and inspire
To look after you
To support you
If I have failed
Forgive me for this
But there is still time
To address feelings and emotions
To correct wrongs of the past
For future progress
To instil hope and trust
Between mother and daughter
Is a challenge I will face
As I feel it is owed to you
Love, respect and friendship

Mother

Labelling

Labels confine
They do not define
In some arenas they dwell
On a negative slant
Attach blame and caution
Isolation and shame
They introduce bias
An ignorance of sorts
Look beyond the label
You may be surprised
By the many facets that unfold
Before your now open eyes
No longer use labels to summarise
An individual's character
Is just as it says
Unique in comparison
Whether for or against
It's usually the latter
When it comes to mental health
The term service user
Is laden by choice
And dependent on service
For one choice, there is little
Whilst compelled to receive
And the baggage attached
The stigma and attitudes
Govern your acts
Govern your every day
Your life and much more
With connotations applied
Isolation ensues
Are we not all service users
Of some sort or other?
Then why is there a hierarchy
A difference attached
For some who are vulnerable
Through no fault of their own
Whilst on the periphery
From out looking in
With tolerance and understanding
Let the dialogue begin.

The Globalised Child

With globalisation
Comes prosperity and gain
For the children of all nations
Some suffer poverty and pain
Inequality in access
To education and health care
Indifferences at the circumstances
That brought each child there
Their basic needs not being met
A right for every child
Irrespective of the country in which domicile
To celebrate globalisation
Where there is want and poverty
Is a fallacy of mankind
As the children of today
Will be responsible for the future
Do you bequeath them poverty,
Hunger, pain and suffering as a legacy
Or do you bequeath
Prosperity, rights and entitlements
For every child?
The rulers of tomorrow
Are the children of today
Self-fulfilling prophecies of past
Should not govern decisions of today
Let the children of all nations speak
Hear their voice, hear their cry
Invite them to the table
When ready to decide
Put their destiny and future in their hands
Give choice, nutrition and education
Health and skills, the will to learn
treat every child as able
let opportunity be a given
Success an achievable aim
All a must for every child

Progress

Educators, Inventors, Scholars and Scientists
Male and female
Against adversity
Conquering disciplines
From which once excluded
Now showing prowess
And significant contribution
To the rich and vibrant
History of the black population

From bondage to freedom
From prejudice to inclusion
From sorrow to joy
Segregation to union
Martin Luther King had a dream
He gave us a vision
Which generations before him
Laid the foundations of
From emancipation to current legislations

Black talent, skills and intellectual abilities
Have been evident throughout history
And should be celebrated on the occasion
Of Black History Month
Being brought to the attention
Of up and coming individuals
Who need inspiration
To continue the progress of histories past
And bring forth cultural cohesion
From nation to nation

The solitude of silence

Its sanctuary is bliss
Days spent reminiscing
Some regrets, some buts, what if's
Anonymity an armour
To protect from the unknown
What was once a refuge
Is now no longer home
Feeling quite less able
My pain a burning spear
The reaction down my spine and leg
Immeasurable to date
Dwarfs my biology
My pain now a contender
Creating misery for me
Relief is but a fraction
Of the magnitude of mass
That permeates my structure
That which is my body mass
The bulk of my composition
Which exacerbates the pain
Is afforded as the problem
But the pain remains the same
It has not been a constant
But there after certain events
That are by the by
And not the cause
It's my bulk that is the main

The Woman in me (A Hysterectomy)

Confined by my boudoir
Till better and well
In my mind I feel healthy
But my body dictates
The need to rest
To charge energies
As I've used my reserves
With the previous demands
That a profession incurs
There's little oil in the well
But a spill will soon flourish
As from strength to strength
Knowing mother nature has healed and repaired
Has nourished and mended
My recovery continuous
As my biology adapts
To its new composition
And enables ability
To function without loss
Of features that may have made whole
To begin a new journey
Understanding that
The sum of my parts do not alone make me whole
As there are many facets which have yet to unfold
I know I may grieve as a chapter is closed
But look to the creation
To the sum of my part
As a mother I am gifted
With a privileged position
As standing before me a heavenly gift
The result of my labours
Of success and much more
That I had opportunity
I am blessed and thankful for

Dedicated to Tracey

Motherhood – choices

My body is in a state of change
Uncertainty is sure to reign
I am with child and feeling vulnerable too
I need support, care and compassion
I need an environment that will accommodate
My mental well-being and productive state

Christine Khisa

A ward at this time feels alien to me
I'm pregnant and need to be allowed to be
With others of a like mind and condition
To have something in common and receive recognition
That services provided should be specific to all needs
Not alone catering for my mental state
My prenatal condition should be equally served

I should be listened to, I need to be heard
No one knows better how I feel, what I want and need
Granted my judgement at times misconstrued
But when it is not am I asked my views

Listen to the recipients of services provided
In order to cater best for their needs at this time
Reports and studies are commissioned in good will
So give us the feedback and keep us informed
So we too can adhere to the norm
We want to be prepared for this special time ahead
To look back and remember with positive thought
The care and encouragement the services brought
And enjoy this experience that comes not to us all

Motherhood – choices 2

My child is born I've a babe in arms
I wish to nurture, bond and calm
But I am not alone at this poignant time
I'm being observed around the clock
They're expecting the worst which is what I am not

Under observation
Not free to act
In a manner according this special event
When I may be naturally high
Buzzing with excitement
But will this be misconstrued
As symptomatic of my condition
Therefore rendering me open to speculation
Is my mental health in need of attention?

Please do not forget
I've just had a baby
My hormones are raging
I'm happy and sad, also both at one time
I'm coming to terms with this change in my life

I need to feel free to express my emotions
And feel safe that there will be no connotations
Leave my mental illness out of the equation
And please focus on my post-natal condition
Let this be paramount just for this instance

Mother

In times of sadness you bring us joy
The foundation of the family
You stabilise and unite

The bond that calms through difficulty
Welcoming children with open arms
There to nurture keep from harm

You teach and educate
Lessons in life
Protect, shield and enable
Our potential you help us to realise

You help us keep our faith
At times when we doubt
You are a friend in deed
When we feel left out

There is no one of you better than any other
You are all special
And today the nation celebrates you 'Mother'
Not only on the day of Mother's Day, but every other
HAPPY MOTHER'S DAY

So Strong

Of you I am so proud
You have conquered a great deal
You have come a long way
Your strength and resolve
Have cushioned your falls
You have stood by your decisions
Made choices you have followed through
I would welcome the opportunity
To celebrate your achievements
To be by your side
When the going gets tough
To suggest to enable
The dreams and plans you have made
To discuss the everyday things
That a mother and daughter relationship obeys
Walk arm in arm down the street
My heart reduces to pieces
As I long for that day when we will be
It's a dream I have yet to fulfil
A longed for reality
A part of me is missing
A void decades in depth
There's still much that's unknown
Like what makes you happy?
What makes you sad?
Your favourite colour
The best toys you had
Your favourite birthday
Who is your best friend?
I feel I know so little
Of yesteryear and yesterday

But I hope that we will have the opportunity
To be mother and daughter once again
And be part of a family
Where there is love there is hope
Where there is faith there is a chance
Whenever you are ready do not hesitate
I'll be there as I have always been
No longer in the shadows
But not maybe able to demonstrate
All the things you long for in a mother
I am beginning to learn
What is sometimes taken for granted
Has to be earned
I've still a long way to go
On this journey of recovery
I hope you will join me
As there is strength in numbers
As mother and daughter the world is our oyster
A force to be reckoned with
No challenge can withhold
The successes we deserve as the next chapter in our
lives together unfold
Forever & always
Mother

Who am I?

I live to love to laugh to smile
To catch the wind to wish a while
To rear to nurture babes in arms
The produce of my loves of past
Of carefree days of health of youth

I long for those days back again
When times were good and friends were friends
Now a statistic of an unwanted kind
To be ignored or pushed aside
By what were once friends and family
Some, now a vague memory

Am I such an embarrassment, such a thorn
To attract ridicule or even scorn?
I'm just as talented as you, or them or they
I too have potential I wish to realise
To encourage to partake
To be part of the equation
In the result have a stake
To be part of society
A link in the chain
Of progress and success
To conquer to hail

My Depression

I feel afflicted, I feel betrayed
My life abandoned, my hopes delayed
This darkness covers me
My sorrow swallows me
My depression moves in slow motion
As if to maximise my suffering

41

I ask why me?

What have I done to deserve this punishment

That makes life so hard to bear

And leaves me constantly living in fear of the next pain?

I could turn to the bottle

To drown my sorrows

Or take my life

End all tomorrows

No! I want to be strong

I have a child to think of

I should fight this depression

From each episode learn a lesson

As the months go by

I no longer feel the need to cry

Established bonds with family, a circle of friends

My books, my music, writing my thoughts unburden me

A belief in oneself, enabled by others has captured
some dignity

These are tools that will conquer the depression that at
this moment is not mine

I now welcome my tomorrows

Christine Khisa

Untitled

I feel alone, rejected, neglected

Depression isolates me

Darkness enters me

I do not want the nights to end

As daylight is not my friend

People speak but I do not hear

I try to think but cannot remember

I look about me and see constant reminders

Of the way things used to be

Of all the promises, hopes and my dreams

I cry for help but nobody hears

I cry till the salt stained streaks appear

I wipe them away before anyone sees

When will this misery leave me

To move on, to start again, to begin

To see the real me, to make friends?

1987

identity

I want to belong

But am really confused

My multiple roles

Cause chaos in my life

At times I am accepted

At others despised

I wear different caps

Depending on the situation

On the company concerned

And there persuasion

It is alright to be me

With bipolar and all

With my 'othering' ethnicity

Single parent and all

Illegitimate children

Through no fault of their own

Will society accept them

Will it condone

There are many paths I have taken

I have some regrets

But what I would not change

Is the pleasure I have met

Many positive roles

Agony aunt still to some

Best of all

Is the acceptance of friends

Who know of the challenges faced

And are never judgemental

Only supportive

To them I'm not mental

Bipolar and I

When neither high
When neither low
I need an equilibrium I'm told
To be able to function
And maintain my position
When high I'm elated
Unrealistic at times
Have high expectations and delusions
I soon come down with a bump
A polarised drop
To the depths of depression
To a place I would not
Wish on a worst enemy
If there was one that was had
The battle and turmoil
That consumes my emotions
And lessens the spoils
Life seems meaningless
Days a mere existence
Nights and endless journey
Into oblivion
When daybreak falls
The sequence continues
For an end to this chapter
I always yearn
I cannot see a better day
As pessimism consumes
Optimism eludes me
The cycle is ending
A balance is reached
I'm at my equilibrium
I've reached my peak
My bipolar recedes
Bipolar and I

Mania

I feel elated on cloud nine
The world's my oyster
There's nothing but time
Enough to do all and achieve all
I'm invincible, there's nothing that I cannot do
I can achieve the impossible
I'm an inventor too
I'm a scholar, I'm important
I have status, I have power
I'm not shy, no more a coward
I'm an extrovert I cannot hide
I'm excited by all the possibilities that are to unfold
I feel elated on cloud nine
The world's my oyster
There's nothing but time
To do all that I wanted to do
No fear of authority, there are no rules
There's just an endless surge of energy
My mind is racing with knowledge to be freed
I know it all
There's nothing beyond me
I feel elated on cloud nine
The world's my oyster
There's nothing but time

The past laid to rest

The inner child in me
Is longing no more
At last I have experienced serenity
My ghosts I've explored
The imagery and sounds
Of the past no longer haunt
The inner child who was so distraught
That child has grown
To a woman, a mother, an aunt, a sister, a great aunt, a partner
That child has been able to conquer her fears
To question the doubts
That allayed her fears
To relinquish memories
That stunted emotional growth and maturity
Allowing for acquaintances
To encourage and inspire
To compliment and praise
That said child's desires
To write, to be read to
To educate, to inform
To communicate through poetry
A medium found to be her norm
To learn from experiences
To acknowledge the pain
But also to know
How to deal with crisis
To turn pain from the past to knowledge
To enable the journey of others
Whilst rearing and nurturing
Role modelling my young
This child's had a journey
That as an adult I have just begun
I'll take the rein in both hands
And strive to do my best
I'll attempt to do the utmost
As of my past I feel cheated
So I've time to make up
And right wrongs for myself
Is closure enough?
My inner child
Has now grown up

Christine Khisa

I want that job

You look through the papers
See the position
You know you can do it
You've got what it takes
But getting the job
There's so much at stake
You fill in the forms
Are shortlisted too
Attend the interview
The best is all you can do
Then there's the dreaded health questionnaire
A million ticks
Yes, I've been there
It's let me down yet again
I've been depressed
I've got a mental health condition
I have Bipolar
I've had admissions
It's all going downhill
The offer's withdrawn
At least I got thus far
It's back to the drawing board once more

You look through the papers
There are vacancies galore
You know you can do it
You've got what it takes
Is there anyone out there
Who's looking to find
An honest hardworking individual, the enthusiastic kind
Who will be loyal and thankful
For the responsibility given
For the opportunity afforded
To earn a living
To contribute, to support
To finance one's life
All I want is a job
To show I too am worthwhile

Communication?

Mixed messages

A chain of whispers

Lack of communication

Unwarranted gestures

Tension, animosity

Of histories past

Ghosts once laid to rest

Resurrected a farce

Drama and conflict

Gossip and friction

Factual context

Deleted for fiction

At the expense of some

For the amusement of others

The price left to pay

The exclusion, the 'other'

Assumptions (A conversation with myself)

You do not look but just assume
You feel you have the right
Through the misconceptions you suppose
Through ignorance and lack
Knowing the comfort of an underdog
Empowers some, I hope not too many
Knowing there is someone lower
In the social strata than yourself
Makes the suffering you suffer
More achievable than wealth
Makes for a false degree of superiority
A form of ignorance itself
You do not question what you see
You do not challenge what society dictates
You do nothing more than accept your fate
Complain when you suffer the consequences
Of the choices that you make
A lack of application of what variable is to blame
Cast a vote and be accountable
If you feel a difference can be made
There are futures here at stake
Grasp every opportunity
May they be fortunate to come your way
Help others who will take the path
On your much trodden road
Lighten the loads of individuals
In countries in which you reside
Enrich your localities with your talents
Know your neighbours and families
From them draw your strength
Recapture the essence of community
That was present yesteryear
Take pride in any position you may hold
And encourage the young
That they too may be so bold.

A conversation with my father

Of you dear father you never told me how men could be
That they could break hearts take hearts
Take away my liberty
You never told me what to expect
You set a standard that I have not yet met

As you were is how I thought they might be
A role model, provider, educator, guardian
Uniting the family through good and bad times
Guiding us through adolescence, a challenging feat
But you stood by us when possible, kept us away from the
streets

I learned sometimes the hard way
My lessons took many a day
Before your wisdom shone through
And gave better days

Though no longer with us
I want you to know
You have instilled in your daughter
What your grandchildren will know
That strength through adversity
Comes from within
But the preparation, the foundation
Are made as you grow
Into the person to make your parents proud
Also others I am sure
Instilling in others qualities admired
Remembered with fondness
Gone but not forgotten

The legacy of knowledge
Gave me a start
But the subject of relationships
Never entered the discussion
So now with my children
I will know to have this conversation

Sunset

As I watch the sunset
I'll reflect if I may
The vast expanse of an orange sky
The vibrant mood and atmosphere
A deserted beach
Warm sand between my toes
The sea glistens
As shadows dance on the surface
As the sun rises
above the horizon
In the distance an area is enveloped
With an orange and blue symmetry
As I look to my left and right
Distance is an eternity
The motionless sea
Vessels moored in a harbour nearby
To capture such a peaceful time
To witness it so grand
This picturesque serenity
Captured on many canvasses
But to capture in my mind
An accessible thought
A memory
I wish never to forget

A change of scene

Time to unwind

Recharge energies

Alleviate stress and negativities

To ponder one's thoughts

To recollect my wishes

To chart progress

And see the aims I have fulfilled

The remainder to be left

For the many moments still

A chance to be happy

Without particular cause

Moments of elation

Freedom from stresses of the past

To that it was never ending

And that those feelings would last

Until the next time that I have a change of scene

I'll have this to look forward to

Until then I'll just dream

Out of town

The drive down
The scenery picturesque
The air seems fresher
With every breath you take
It may be imagined
I do not know
But when I am out of town I seem to flourish
Green fields for miles
Some with crops, some livestock
A pleasure to view
As opposed to a tower block
The contrast is unexplainable
The difference imaginable
What it does for me
The journey alone is to change my mindset
And capture much that is rare in my life
When I leave the chaos of the metropolis
For a place where pace is serene
The atmosphere tranquil
Like I have experienced in a dream
Remembering days when I played in neighbouring
streets
Fond memories of carefree days
With little responsibilities
To weigh my day
To revisit these places
To show respect to the past
Laying down old ghosts
That the present had masked
I have found a new freedom
That I hope will last
And give me a chance to respect and learn
That yesteryear and yesterday
Can make way for today and tomorrow

The colour green

It's calming, soothing
Inviting, enveloping, protecting
Serene is green
Fresh and vibrant
A field of green is wonderfully exciting
A meadow, a lawn, a field would welcome me
To bask in the glory of another day
With rays from the sun
Comforting me with warmth
The scent of the bluebells
Aromas galore
I would like to stay
In this wondrous place
What the colour green
Signifies for me
Is hope eternal and longevity
Tranquillity, a colour that makes me feel free
Inspires me to write
Encourages me to think
To express myself
Helps me to be me
The colour green

A Carer needs care too

An obligation, a duty
Sometimes a double edged sword
When your strengths is depleted
And the demands are much more

Who cares for the Carers
These invisible champions
Who replenish the finance
Of government hoards

Balancing The Scales

By minimising the expense of the ones they care for
By assuming responsibility
Of loved ones, family and friends
Always on duty, the care never ends

Both children and adults
Are carers alike
With responsibilities beyond
What the services might

A carer has compassion
Patience and understanding
Sometimes not by choice does the position unfold
But out of necessity
To keep loved ones in the fold

Young carers too also need support
So they can look back on their childhood
And not feel denied
The experiences of their peers
And look back on their childhoods
With memories full
Of challenges they conquered
To care for those most dear
Whilst still enjoying childhood
With support given
Being educated to grow
Into upstanding individuals
Who have made a contribution so great
That financial recompense
Would only underestimate

They will have a perspective on caring
That cannot be given
It has to be lived
As carers never stop giving
Who cares for the carers?

Our bodies are important too!

Our bodies are important too
The physical and the mental of equal value
To reach a balance
Address all concerns
Then a more holistic approach will begin to emerge

A pain in my back
No, it is not stress
No need to review medication
It's not all in my head

To neglect my physical needs does me long term no
justice
It should be reviewed equally
Look to the cause of my symptoms
Do not misconstrue them with my psychiatric condition

We'll achieve a healthier community
When services meet all of our needs
By working more in conjunction, GP's and CMHT'S

Referring when necessary our physical ailments
So they too can be met
And good health can prevail

Physically healthier having had needs met
More able to actively engage in community life and
events
Is a contribution that will enhance
The service user profile

Being involved in your own care

I want the chance to make decisions
That will eventually reduce admissions
A chance to discuss and alternate my care
When the initial solutions are not working well

On medication, I'm not the best informed
But give me more information, direct me to a source
I am at the centre of my well-being
I am the patient, I wish the best for myself and others
alike

If I do not involve myself in my care
It's hard to complain
I just have to adhere
There is need to be pro-active and take some charge
Of decisions made on my behalf

It will impact on other areas in my life
Increase confidence, assertiveness and self esteem
Working in partnership with GP's and C.M.H.T.'s

Regular contact, discussions and communication
Respect for my opinion will enhance my co-operation
And put me in an advantageous position

To take the reins, put order in my life
Give me the choice that will help me to strive
To be part of the community accepted like any other
To be seen to be normal, productive and worthwhile
And condition relapse not a permanent state
But mental well being a success to celebrate

Christine Khisa

Moving forward together

With every action, every step
Our partnership strengthens
Service user, service provider, carers and professionals
With participation, collaboration and negotiation

Hearing the views of those concerned
Giving forums and platforms so that we too can learn
How to better the process pathways and experiences
Of those our service is destined for and their families
And the services providers who meet their needs

To take on board suggestions, comments, compliments
and complaints
To create opportunities, well being and understanding
The paths our journeys take are destined to meet on the
road ahead

There is need to capture further
The wealth of experience, creativity and knowledge
Of recipients of our services
To embrace change and development
Enhancing what already exists
To build on the strength of partnerships
Enabling opportunities whilst combating stigma
Exploring innovative ideas
And in so doing achieving a common goal
Moving forward together

Know yourself, love yourself, as you love life

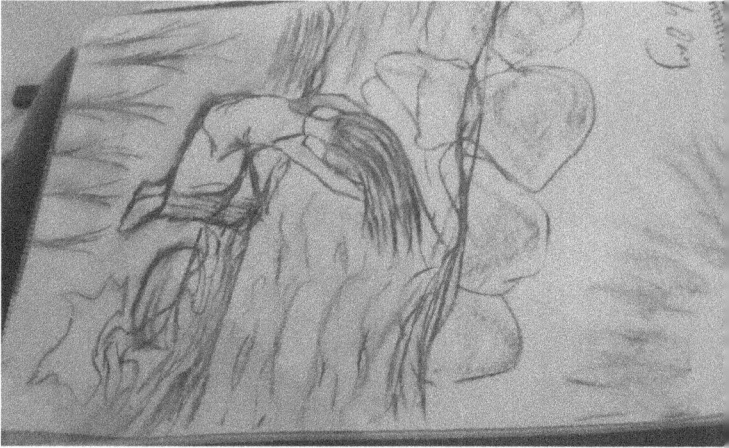

You need not always be strong
Know that illness is no sign of weakness
It is fine for others to lend support
Seek help when you feel the need
When in pain feel free to cry out
Consult your GP when in doubt
To address ill health and avoid neglect
You bring your loved ones a chance of hope
That they will never regret
A chance to celebrate your recovery
A chance to show how much you are admired
Without this chance pride and ignorance can take its
place
Decide, should they mourn your loss or celebrate
That you challenged breast cancer and fought back
That you attempted to conquer a major concern
And welcomed the support that came forth in return
Take time to be dependent on others

Mothers, fathers, sisters, brothers, husbands, friends
and colleagues will understand
And from at least one of the above
will come a helping hand
To support you through times when you want to give up
To celebrate when you know the worst is behind you
Love yourself as you love others
Because self neglect is an injustice like no other
You are the roots of your community
Without you it will not flourish
And the foundations you have worked on
May no longer be nourished
As in your absence everyone will blame themselves
That they did not do enough to support your health
That they took advantage of your generous nature
And neglected to ask
How you were, how you felt, have you had any rest?
When did you last have a check up or a routine test?
Questions hardly ever asked but with the best of
intentions
Until we start asking we are doing our women a
disservice
Someone will lend an ear
Ask yourself, ask others, enquire and confide
Your doubts and your fears, seek reassurance
From those best placed to provide a solution
And the care and concern for what could be a potential
problem
If left unaddressed and put aside
Take charge of your destiny
Take control of your life

Obesity (The Size of Me)

When you see me you see my size
Do you see the qualities it hides?
Does society maximise my potential
Or sit in judgement on the differential
My size as with many is not all of my own doing
My metabolism is irate
Affected by the medication I take
For twenty years or more
My consumption is dictated by my condition
When given a prescription I was not informed
That my size may alter, be other than the norm
They say you are what you eat
Does this go for medication?
If this is true
Do we real know the true extent of the situation?
I've been mourning for years
The effects of my 'meds' but I suppose it was thought
It was all in my head
But now there is investment, now there is concern
When the problems in crisis to it attention is turned
My rate of consumption is out of control
But I attempt to fight back
As a struggle unfolds
Do not just see my size
See beyond, understand
That I too have feelings
And need recognition
Of a condition that affects many in a similar situation
Please do not rule us out of the equation.

Nubian

An Empress to all, Object of desire,

The ability to nurture, The will to inspire,

Your presence is witnessed globally,

Your influence international,

You penetrate every entity with the resonance of your being,

You are history in the making, with many given meanings

Your strength through adversity, the back bone of your brothers, your sons, their fathers, your husbands, your lovers

Nubian, Empress, Queen, Princess,

Titles you have held with grace and prowess,

Your strengths unfold with wisdom and age,

For the younger generation,

The cultural capital in the knowledge you instil

is more rewarding than materialism left in a will

We are a people of many cultures, languages, faiths, beliefs and traditions

these variables give us our identity but can also give us unity

where society may manipulate them to segregate

we are a force to be reckoned with, a people of conscience

Nubian woman you are in a position to dictate

And create the path the next generation take

Leave your mark in history

Let the stories that are handed down

Be of the achievement of you and me

This poem is dedicated to my three daughters

Nasimiyu, Nakhanu, Muhindi and my son Simiyu.

Success

How do you chart success, is it by praise or wealth

By recommendation, recognition, or believing in
oneself?

Success from within knows no bounds and will unfold

Through the deeds that you do for yourself and for
others

No one can chart your progress better than you who are
about to discover

Your strengths and your talents, your wisdom and your
presence

Believing in yourself is an untold wealth that will lead
you to success

That comes in many forms, for every individual there are

Different norms, different values, different goals

Success is personal, but can be shared if you wish

To encourage and enable others, to join the journey

Which may at times have obstacles

But with faith and conviction you will conquer all hurdles

And achieve respect, dignity and understanding

Affording the success you deserve

Christine Khisa

Take Courage

Black men stand up, take your place
There is a platform that you must grace
Your battle with society may be never ending
But your solutions to the problem
Could be the start of new beginnings

Mentor your young
Role model the adolescent
Draw an experience of your fathers
And forefathers from generations past
Always bear in mind the struggles
Of those who laid the foundations

Reward their legacy by doing your part
However big however small
A contribution is a start
To add to the many histories
That will be told of you and your sons
Your women bare the burdens of many injustices
The adaptability resonates in their prowess
They can manipulate a problem
And achieve a positive outcome
Be subtle and tactile with an air of diplomacy

The strengths are within you; release them and grow
Into the stature and position
That nature bestowed
It is only natural that you should expect
To be equally adorned with position and success
And be a credit to your people
You should aim for the best.

Gratitude

I am thankful, I am blessed
For what I have got
As I remember the days
When I had not
When I suffered in silence
Being too proud to ask
Being ashamed of my failures
Of mistakes of the past
Ashamed of my condition
And the stigma it drew
The isolation, the segregation
The nothingness to look forward to

Now in a better place
My experiences I have put to rest
From them I have learnt many lessons
On how to deal with future challenges
And if on the way
I can assist others in a similar predicament
I will feel honoured to be asked
To share knowledge I have gained
To make other people's recovery
Less turbulent than mine
Though every journey differs
Experience is valuable
And allows others the time
To focus on the positive things in life
That many take for granted
Being a service user is no longer a sentence
But an opportunity to influence, educate and show
That throughout our experiences
There are semblances of normality that we too hold
I am thankful every day I am well
As I do not know what tomorrow holds
Bipolar is unpredictable
And all of life's triggers I do not know

Beginnings/Choices

You were not a doctor or a lawyer born

But a babe in arms as I once was

Life chances threw the die for our destinies

Choices to be had but for a few

Denied for many, our paths misconstrued

Do we come to terms or admit defeat?

Accepting our conditions may render our choices
obsolete

But for opportunities that have not arisen

From recognition of our worth and inclusion

No longer worthless no more exclusion

We are part of society and need to stake our claim

As part of a system, we too should reign

We have a voice and need to be heard

We need to be recognised for our total worth

When decisions are made

Include us in the process

When employing, include us in the quotas

To create well being, tolerance and understanding

Make sure service users to have a hand in

Life Chances

Spare me your pity
For I have lived
The life society was destined to give
One with no voice
No opinion, no choice
Invisibly suffering
Immersed in trauma and pain
Of a guilt ridden past
Of which I was not to blame
The subject of ridicule, resentment and scorn
If life was a chess board
I am but a mere pawn
Of us there are many
In the lower strata we reside
In the upper echelons of power
They ignore our demise
These may be but mere ramblings
Of my demented thoughts
But to place them in reality
Would be an awakening of sorts
Freedom, love, respect and equality
Variables I have yet to experience
Lest I be granted longevity
Man's inhumanity to man is now a given
Take from life what you will
Disregard those less fortunate
Let their suffering be in vain
It is not your problem
Lest the butterfly effect
Globally redistribute the balance of wealth
And you walk in the shoes
Of someone with less than yourself.

Is It Real

When life's so good
And you look forward to another day
When you want for nothing
And you are financially secure
When the children do their homework
When you gain job satisfaction
When you pass your assignments
On a course that you took
When family come together
And there is nothing but harmony
These are the days I wished for
And now they are happening to me
I give thanks every day
And take nothing for granted
As there have been days
When I would give up
Because the stress was too much
My depression was dark
My moods up and down
I felt so isolated
I walked with my head down
I now hold my head up high
The sky is my limit
If you are reading this poem
I have achieved a goal
Just sharing my story
It's heartfelt to know
That others will read it
And have similar thoughts
To know that life's journey
Is sometimes full of surprises
And that we all have potential
We need a way to maximise
But for some special individuals
Who I would like to acknowledge for giving me a chance
An opportunity, a solution, encouragement and much more
I feel honoured to be in the company of those who inspired me
And strengthened my weaknesses
Built up my confidence
Brought out the real me
Lord I thank you
For me being me

Loss

There's so much I have forgotten and taken for granted
The loss of a father
Coming to terms with reality
Distance has made it easier to bear
Living in different countries
Softened the blow
But knowing that I'll be fatherless
Is a situation I am still coming to terms to know
Blurred memories
Confused conversations
Muddled recollections
Of how things used to be
As time passes, life goes on
Life is for the living
For those who have passed on you cherish the memories
Whether good or bad
Even something vague gives respect to their having been
The patriarch of the family
Through formative years and beyond
A father figure is important in a family
And should be a foundation
It should nurture and instil
Values and traditions
Respect, confidence and honesty in any given situation
This may be an idealistic view of a father figure
It's what I would have wished for given the choice
For the children that I have
Whom I have reared alone
As fathers can solidify the family
And from the outside and unknown
They too can protect, provide and care for
And leave us with memories
That are not hard to recollect
But will be passed on to our children
Lest they be denied
The privilege of a father
Should be a right for every child.

Maasai

Like a warrior you stand so tall
You demand from mother nature just enough not all
In harmony with mother earth
In the motherland your place of birth
Age old skills still serve you well
Traditions instilled in your offspring as well
A people of stature
At one with the elements
No bulk buying, hoarding, waste or indulgence
You live according to your means
As nature intended
In the Motherland AFRICA
Pay homage to your Queens
The guardians of your children
Who carry on your dreams

The Residue

What I am left with

What I have to fulfil

The void in this entity

The hurt that makes it bleak

The confusion that ensues

Being misunderstood is too much

Want and envy

Lack and pride

The meaning of friends and family pushed aside

Picked up when needed

Ignored when of no use

Being treated like an object

Of limited purpose

The sanctuary of silence

The solitude of stillness

No explanation needed

At peace with myself

This period is over

Till the next time I'll brace myself

This Demon Depression

Silent pain, anguish, fear

Invisible suffering when company is near

The mask of confidence

To allay concerns

Is beginning to crack as the pressure unfolds

This demon depression

Is taking hold

When vulnerable through external stress

My defences are weakened

I feel my stability crumble

This time for the depression I am no match

To do a good deed

And to have it rebuffed

To reach out the hand of friendship

But it is not enough

You can't change the hurt

Or take away the misery

You can't change the past

You can't alter your destiny

With strength from my faith

A crutch by my side

I'll not venture into darkness

As I have in times gone by

The Lord is my shepherd

He will be by my side

Many times I have doubted

And lost my faith

This time I'll persevere

My options are few

When this episode is over

I'll look back and reflect

And hope it's the last time

Depression and I have met

To Eternity

I thought I would love you to eternity
Then you broke my heart
And crushed my faith in you
All the trust that I'd instilled in our relationship
Meant nothing in a moment of weakness
You gave me no respect
I thought I'd love you to eternity
Trust, faith, honour, unity
Things that had built up over time
Reduced to nothing
No evidence of them ever having existed
What were you thinking of?
Were your thoughts that twisted?
I have now moved on
In a safer place
Free from the emotional turmoil
I mistook for love
Free from the burden
Of unrequited love
I can stand by my own conviction
Be assured by my decisions
I have faith in myself
My confidence has grown
I am a woman of substance
It's a shame you will never know

Christine Khisa

Tranquillity

Serene surroundings, utopian thoughts

A world with no envy, with poverty at nought

Peace a commonality, communication is universal

Eliminated are the boundaries

Love and hope transcends what were once barriers

Trust is now commonplace

Freedom when expressed through thought and deeds

Are complimented with success

Success in love, life, work, faith and family

All this I hope will one day be commonplace

We live in a world with many problem populations

Where wealth and knowledge are polarised

Our hierarchy of needs never reaches self actualisation

Our wants never satisfied, we eke out a mere existence

But for thoughts of tranquillity

There is hope yet to our being

Horizon (Bereavement)

To watch a boat sailing from a distant shore

To breathe the sea air a pleasure once more
The shadows dance on the waves as they rise
I look up to the distant clouds in the sky

On the horizon where the two great entities meet
The sea and the sky like old friends greet
To be a guest at that meeting, what a story to tell
A moment of pleasure that none can excel

As the soft white sand runs through my toes
And cushions my step with every stride I take
With the warmth from the sun, the freshness from the
sea
I could bathe in the silk like sand
And soak in the warm soothing sensuous waves
I could day dream for hours as I absorb the atmosphere
Not wanting it to end
For time to stand still
It would be grander than grand

The sky darkens, the waves become fierce
The sand is claimed back by the incoming tide
My encounter must end due to the grandmaster – time
Until another day, God blessed countless ahead
I will visit this place, but my memories will stay
Always with me be it morning or night
Whether happy or sad the experience shared
With one other than myself will once again take me
there

My 'Pandora's Box'

The box that is Pandora's
Once opened cannot be closed
Once licensed to the contents
What does her future hold?
As time is the Grandmaster
With little time left in the day
Consumed with pain and tragedy
There has been little gain
If one could close the box and turn back time
Would be a wish in the making
This cruel world and cruel life
Everything is for the taking
The streets are bleak
The air is cold
The atmosphere I have yet to mention
Oh to be but somewhere else
Would be heaven in the making
All my years
Both child and grown
Confined by geography
Defined by my condition
Also my biology
I do not speak
Just watch and learn
Observe and reserve judgement
As whilst imposed upon myself
Am aware of all the consequence
The burdens of the chains I bear
The weight the years amass
My character, my individuality
A fragment of the past
If my life were but a puzzle
The centre piece has not been found
Puzzle incomplete
I admit defeat
And put my destiny in your hands
Those who decide how sane I am
My medication and much more
Those who decide
Script my day, my month, my year, my life
My 'Pandora's Box' is yours

Christine Khaemba Khisa is of Kenyan parentage, born in London in 1964 one of eight siblings, now a mother of 4. She has been a client of Mental health and Social Care Services for over 25 years.

Christine has worked in a paid and voluntary capacity for SLaM Mental Health Foundation Trust since 2005. She has also completed and later delivered a Service User 'Train the Trainers' course equipping participants with the skills to design and present training, also enabling fellow service users to structure their narratives to achieve the maximum potential in creating mental health awareness in voluntary, statutory and community settings.

Christine held the position of Service User Involvement Co-ordinator for SLaM NHS Trust, for a few years, whilst in post in 2009 developed and managed with supervision 'The Peer Storytelling Sessions', which arose from an idea from a Service User in relation to how information was disseminated. The project was an innovative method of peer to peer involvement sharing recovery narratives within an inpatient setting, then further afield to statutory and community settings.

Christine has also been an active member of the User participation forum at Middlesex University and London South Bank University, she has been part of a steering group promoting and developing creative learning materials using 'arts as a medium for dialogue and transition', Christine has been co-published and has co-presented to various institutional forums on these projects.

Christine has a BSc in Social Sciences gained through The Open University and intends to pursue further education. Here interests include articulating her experiences through creative writing and poetry, clothing design, reading self help literature, charcoal sketching and music.

www.ingramcontent.com/pod-product-compliance
Lightning Source LLC
Chambersburg PA
CBHW031218270326
41931CB00006B/612